CW00665548

Full Advance Praise for
Renzo Del Castillo's *Still*

"These are the kind of poems that will inspire you to write, and the kind that you will return to, again and again. Renzo Del Castillo paints landscapes of memories and cities in such a way that you feel as if you are reading a photograph that was taken at just the right moment." — Tiffiny Rose Allen, Author of *At The Beginning Of Yesterday*

"Renzo Del Castillo's *Still* takes your heart on a dreamy romantic ride through exotic landscapes, like Montmartre, Antigua, Lisbon and Bali, to show you all the different kinds of love we may be lucky to experience in our lifetime. It is hands-down one of the most inspiring poetry books I have read in a long time. I couldn't put it down." — Annie Vazquez, Author of *My Little Prayer Book: 75 Prayers, Poems and Mantras for Illumination*

"Renzo Del Castillo's debut *Still* takes readers on a profound, sepia-toned, nostalgic journey through the interconnectedness of self-discovery. Acknowledge the inherent absurdity of love at first sight while embracing the transformative potential that meeting someone holds as well as the evocative feelings of culture and familial ties in this captivating collection." — Oscar Fuentes, Author of *Honey & Sting*

"*Still* is a beautiful, lyrical collection of poetry that pays homage to the motherland and the trials and tribulations that come with life experiences such as immigrating to a new country, finding and losing love, and experiencing travel and what the world has to offer. Complete with poems translated to both French and Spanish, Still is a love letter to memory, to adapting to new cultures, and to viewing the world through a new lens." — Flor Ana, Author of *A Moth Fell In Love With The Moon*

STILL

RENZO DEL CASTILLO

Cover Art Copyright © 2023 by Renzo Del Castillo
Edited by Flor Ana Mireles

1st Edition | 01
Hardcover ISBN: 979-8-9880379-9-6

First Published July 2023

For inquiries and bulk orders, please email:
indieearthbooks@gmail.com

Printed in the United States of America 1 2 3 4 5 6 7 8 9

Available in Paperback:
979-8-9880379-8-9

Indie Earth Publishing Inc.
| Miami, FL |

www.indieearthbooks.com

INDIE EARTH
PUBLISHING

STILL

Renzo Del Castillo

To my mother, Rosario Moreno, for teaching me to love; to my father, Ernesto Del Castillo, for teaching me to believe; and to my sister, Maria Wilmoth, for teaching me to be kind.

"Poetry is what happens when nothing else can."
— Charles Bukowski

"He who does not travel, who does not read,
who does not listen to music,
who does not find grace in himself,
dies slowly."
— Pablo Neruda

"You can find the entire cosmos lurking
in its least remarkable objects."
— Wislawa Szymborska

Foreword
By Curtis Franklin, Jr.

Rain pours down on a Florida night; sounds through closed windows mix with muffled drops on a weather-tight roof. The smell of the rain is a welcomed perfume, scenting the heavy feel of humid air on skin. If you live in the tropics, you know these sensations, know that they're markers of home.

In this collection of work, there are the markers of life made vivid and real through words of poems, disciplined and wild, focused and expansive, in the language of Miami. Miami dances through these pages in poems and passages of English, Spanish, and both. More than a place, in Renzo's work, it is a ground on which life is drawn.

Still, like the layered grounds on which it lives, is strong and deep. Family is the deepest ground, the foundation that allows a life to soar, and soar it does. And that is what makes this collection so worthwhile. When poetry and a life are deserving of one another, readers are given permission to travel into that life, expanding and enriching their own lives by the light of the now-revealed truth.

The work in this book was not possible before now. The work needed a life for birth—a life in full, with so many possibilities realized—and so many more waiting for their moment. It has been a life that demanded to be expanded into poetry, a life that has been shared with so many while waiting to be shared in the language contained between these covers.

Renzo has been part of my life for many years—a part that has made all the other parts better, richer, more alive. And so, the poems I found when I read *Still* were not surprising—they come from his remarkable life force. And yet... These words focus that force in powerful, new ways firmly rooted in a history that extends back beyond his birth to the roots of his family and life. In so many ways, you read these words alone and part of a chorus of voices distilled in Renzo's singular timbre.

So, read. And as you read, hear the rhythm of the words. Feel the music. Feel the life in the language. When you feel the warm drops of a storm that did not rain on your skin, you will understand.

Quietud:

Sobre un libro. Sobre la poesía. Sobre la amistad.

By Íñigo de Amescua Fernández de Casadevante

Jamás he estado en Lima. Todo tiene sus comienzos. Uno siempre es varias personas al mismo tiempo. Todos tenemos que asumir que nuestros rasgos físicos, nuestras emociones, las pupilas, los dedos, se metamorfosean ante lo que tenemos delante. Somos sepias de dos piernas y mil sentimientos arremolinados en la cabeza, el pecho, la tripa. Somos un coche en una carretera de montaña, sin conductor, persiguiendo algo que una vez soñamos siendo niños. Algunos son una nómina, otros son garrapatas anaranjadas, otros plantas rodadoras, otros cantos rodados. Unos son Cortázar, otros Henry Miller. Zombis, cantantes de blues, pescadores. Conductores de tren, astronautas, equilibristas. Caciques de pueblo, engañabobos, saltimbanquis. Unos Rolling Stones, otros Camarón. Caraduras, yonkis, predicadores, mitómanos, malabaristas. Unos son niños mimados que te empujan y desean atención, otros son el niño callado, gordito y solitario que sueña con jugar en Maracaná. El superhéroe sin capa, el que se queda dormido en el concierto, el que salva el mundo, el que acaba con él.

En este libro hay poemas sobre fantasmas, pasión, personas que se te escapan entre los dedos en una nube de Chanel y sudor. Por supuesto, hay amor, pérdida, amargura, frustración. París, Viena, Miami. Está presente la necesidad de formar parte de algo, la necesidad de huir, la mirada atrás que uno lanza sin querer en la pista de un aeropuerto a 80.000 kilómetros de su casa. También hay hogares construidos a tres metros sobre tierra, hogares sin raíces. Hogares que uno forma cuando no es de ningún lado y de varios a la vez. Cuando uno tiene amigos desperdigados por varios sitios, que es lo mismo que decir que tiene el corazón desarmado. Se van poniendo chinitas de piedras en el camino por si acaso, pero la noche es larga y oscura y, a veces, uno se olvida de dónde las puso ¿Quién eres? ¿Dónde estoy?

He tenido el honor de haber podido leer este libro a flashes desde antes de que fuera un libro. Desde antes que nada. Solo destellos de líneas en una conversación por un servicio de mensajería instantánea. Poemas escritos en otros días y otras noches a miles de kilómetros de distancia y enviados, lanzados, quizá, como aviones de papel hacia el otro lado del Atlántico. Ahí se guardaban hasta que yo los viera. En ningún lado. Sobre nuestras cabezas. En el corazón de tierras raras de mi teléfono. Luego yo los leía cuando podía, en el metro, en la terraza, en la calle. Veía, poco a poco, como aquello que Renzo tenía en la cabeza, lo que le quitaba el sueño, lo que le acompañaba cada noche, tomaba forma, ladrillo tras ladrillo y se iba acumulando en algún lugar en su escritorio, en su cabeza, en su memoria. Ahora este libro está entre tus manos y puedes leerlo con toda la tranquilidad del mundo. Puedes ponerlo sobre tu mesilla de noche y mirarlo antes de dormir. Llevártelo de viaje. Ponerlo junto a otros libros, tomar notas, prestárselo a tu hermano, a tu madre, al chico que acabas de conocer y al que te gustaría besar en el cuello tiernamente. Aprovéchalo. Léelo con cuidado, a Renzo hay que leerlo con cuidado porque él escribe así, con cuidado, adrede. A cada autor hay que leerlo así, como sea él, para entenderlo. A veces hay que poner música de fondo, otras hay que llevárselo a un bar, otras a un bosque, otras bajo las sábanas. A Renzo hay que leerlo en silencio, en el lobby de un hotel.

La poesía es mirar con los ojos medio cerrados para dar opción a que las cosas puedan cambiar más fácilmente, ayudar a que muten, se mezclen, se levanten y anden por sí solas. Mirar sus formas cambiantes como en una lámpara de lava. La poesía es intentar fijar todo eso en la mente, acordarse. La poesía es tener siempre un cuadernito y un lápiz cerca. Es estar callado. Es dejarse llevar. Es tener paciencia. Es rezar en la noche a la diosa de la misericordia y acordarse de Leonard Cohen, Basho y Safo. Son las lágrimas de los aqueos en la arena de Ilión la de los altos muros. Es un peregrino refugiado bajo un techo de madera caminando al norte. Es Lorca fusilado por los fascistas por ser homosexual. Dylan Thomas borracho como una cuba; Philip Larkin con su pajarita de hombre aburrido sepultado entre libros; la mirada triste de Pizarnik escribiendo sobre un pizarrón sus últimas palabras: "no quiero ir, nada más, que hasta el fondo."

Renzo no es como yo. Yo no soy como Renzo. De hecho, somos lo opuesto en muchos aspectos. No escribimos igual, no nos expresamos igual. Él tiene método, disciplina, confianza. Renzo es tranquilo, meticuloso, atento, constante. Yo no. Yo admiro eso. Todo esto se lee en cada línea de sus poemas. En los espacios vacíos, en los comienzos, en los fines. Se ve en su vocabulario, en el sonido de su voz trasladado a sus frases. Es patente en sus temas, en sus "I don't believe in love at first sight;" sus "Magdalena feels charcoal tears scald her scarred cheeks," sus "drenched in the Machiavellian philosophy of her sweat" o sus "These things and more fill the room alongside your empty chair." Renzo va formando sus piezas, pensando bien, eligiendo bien, sintiéndose a gusto con lo que hace. Renzo es un agricultor cuidadoso. Mira el cielo, toca la tierra, la riega, planta sus semillas, habla a las plantas, mira al sol. Se oculta de la lluvia en el porche. Elige, crea su tempo, es pulcro, bueno, sentimental. Yo no. Nunca lo seré. Por eso, él ha escrito este libro. Por eso yo sería incapaz de hacerlo.

En estos poemas hay un lugar que se dibuja de manera específica, casi siempre. Puede ser una habitación de hotel, un viaje, un bar, la arena, la calle, Bali, Praga, Lisboa... Sus versos suceden casi siempre en un escenario particular que asienta el tono, la acción, las frases que van cayendo a veces simples, a veces alambicadas sobre las paredes, el suelo, las sillas, las mesas, como si se tratase de una lluvia constante y tupida. Renzo aprende, se habla a sí mismo, se da consejos, mientras escribe. Se recuerda lo importante, las personas, los principios que rigen sus pasos. Se lo dice diciéndolo en voz alta. Lo deja patente en fraseos de tres palabras o en párrafos de 120. Se habla a sí mismo, para aprender a olvidar, para recordar de la manera adecuada, para darse ánimo, para dar un portazo. Aflicción, ausencia, rabia... el amor. Brothers es un ejemplo: "Little brother, disregard your constraints. You find beauty in life when you ignore the ticking clock. Time is ongoing, incomplete, eternal. Experience the passage of time; honor it." Se aconseja, se palpa los bolsillos para comprobar que no se le olvida nada encima de la mesa del salón, en el mueble del recibidor, en la chaqueta. Renzo es bastante budista, aunque no lo sepa. Cualquier persona que aprecia la sabiduría lo es. Epicuro, Diógenes, Zenón de Citio. Céntrate en el ahora, inténtalo, es lo único que tenemos y ya se marcha, rápido, por entre las pestañas.

Por otro lado, este libro no está, en manera alguna, desconectado de estos tiempos. Aquí tenemos la ansiedad, las redes sociales, la distancia, la mutación de las relaciones emocionales, la licuefacción del cariño, el sexo y el amor. Aquí tenemos el desapego, el deseo, la memoria. La ausencia de un dios, la búsqueda, la libertad, el último acto de creación de un posible sentido para aquello que no lo tiene. Renzo es un romántico empedernido que, a veces, se cura y a veces no y esa ingenuidad es una seña que otorga una autenticidad afectiva a todo este libro. "I love you in the way great mysteries are loved: / quietly, with excitement and full of expectations / Curiosity holds court, demanding to know your secrets."

Vivir es muchas veces aprender a manejarte con las ausencias. Uno echa de menos a su madre, a su padre, a su amor de juventud, a su amigo que vive en otro país... o en el tuyo propio, a miles de kilómetros de distancia. Uno, a veces, vive un poco en varios sitios a la vez. No se puede olvidar, es imposible. Te transportas a un taxi en Nueva York hace 15 años. A las montañas del Cáucaso. A una piscina en un motel de Texas. A las ruinas de Pompeya. Al Sena un otoño de hojas caídas y cielos grises cuando estuviste a punto de morir y tu cara en el cristal de un supermercado te asustó porque parecías un cadáver enjuto y afilado como un cuchillo de hueso. Renzo vuelve. Escribe sobre ello. Forma pequeños recuerdos en botellas de cristal que parecen oraciones murmuradas en voz baja. Renzo es un poco un monje franciscano en su celda, en un monasterio, en la llanura. Mira por su ventana y se pregunta por la muerte, su madre, dios ("I kneeled tonight and began to pray / when the question came to mind: 'To whom?'").

Somos tantas cosas... Lo difícil es mantener los ojos bien abiertos bajo la máscara. Renzo los tiene. Este es su libro. Esto es él.

Contents

STILL

Renzo Del Castillo

Beginnings

The runway shrinks;
encasing Vegas into an unseasonable snow globe
while French is whispered loudly across my aisle.
Jet lag joins forces with insomnia and I'm stretched
between two points of an exhausting spectrum.

I can see her,
blurry vision enhancing sight, tears a lens;
her Russian-doll face, all dimples and eyes.
She sits on the pink cushions of her thighs,
wrapped in cotton candy,
comfortably alternating between chewing gum
and twirling her hair into silken spools
on her soft fingers.

The smell of fresh laundry intertwines with Chanel, sweat,
late night movies, and stolen looks in the cafe.
It exfoliates me, her texture tickling my skin;
pore after pore unclogged of whomever touched it last.

I taste her lips,
the flavor rests briefly on my tongue
and spreads down my throat,
morphing from watermelon
to Toblerone.

My own yawning wakes me,
placing me squarely on an aisle seat
in the coach section of a plane dingy enough to be affordable.
The stewardess slams the snack cart into my shoulder,
yelling out her wares for any passenger
foolish enough to spend twelve dollars on a sandwich.

Now, she eludes me.
Like the Cheshire cat,
all that's left behind
are her honeycomb eyes,
until she blinks,
leaving me
without a memory to hold on to,
to fill my senses,
until the warning light turns off.

Butterfly Effect

I've read about love at first sight;
logically, it's absurd, but
whether destiny or coincidence,
I know that meeting you is an opportunity.
I know nothing about you,
except
how your hands will feel in mine,
the way my pillows will absorb the smell of your hair,
how your flip-flops will look strewn on my bedroom floor.

I know just how
your gum wrappers will line my wastepaper basket
and I know the heart-shape your thighs will take
resting comfortably beneath my hoodie.

I am nothing to you now,
but I could be your happiness,
your depression, your excuse to bar-hop on Tuesday nights.
I could be the reason you hurry home,
your co-host for a potluck,
and your joint bank account holder.

Your rebellion against your father,
your best friend's secret crush, your official jar-opener,
your frustration, your alarm clock, your ride to church.
Your blanket, your scapegoat, and your last orgasm tonight.
I can be all that and yours.

Give me your love and your overreactions,
all you have to offer,
and everything you hold back.

Let me weave layer after layer of you
into the fabric of my life,
vibrant and rich textures to warm us both
during the cold and dry February nights ahead.
A cocoon of photographs and stories,
decorated in quaint post-modern sentiment.
The pale halo of your skin in full bloom;
a lamp to light our rainiest afternoons
while Ray LaMontagne strums our story out.
We are an E-minor chord transitioning to an A,
a D chord evolving into G;
we should be.

Join me for afternoons at the pool hall and nights at the cafe,
live jazz highlighting our conversations.
For lakeside barbecues and early morning runs.
For birthdays and family reunions featuring
my aunt's Nutella strawberry cake.
Let me introduce you
to a night walking around Vienna,
to an hour on Parisian backstreets,
to a day spent on the Grecian coast.

Fall into my arms and realize
that you are where you're genetically predisposed to fit;
that there is no other place where you'll be more at home.

No,
I don't believe in love at first sight.
It's absurd,
but I do believe in possibilities.

Naming Constellations

I've worshiped you,
I'm afraid.
I've raised you so high above me
I've made it impossible to reach you.
I can only see you through
the cheap telescope of the imagination;
a trace of a shadow of a light.
You've been gone for over millions of years.

Melatonin Deficiency

It is impossible to name the reasons
that keep me awake at night;
unknown captors of my thoughts,
ransoming peace for forty silver pieces.

Ex-Factor

I can feel restrained love pour from you
with every squeeze of my arm you steal.
Your touch says what you don't dare,
fearful of the confirmation that exists
in the unspoken realm of past regrets.

The torture you must have endured
when the phantom of my words
spoken at the moment of our parting
haunted true, echoing in your ears:
"I would have loved you so much."

Previously published in the Scarlet Leaf Review.

Halloween

Behind the contours of this mask,
almond eyes brand your outline on my memory.
The curves of your body are tattooed
on the back of my desire;
drawing painfully acquired,
inked with passion's blood.

On this old, hallowed night,
where fantasies materialize through costumed dreams
and spirits seek comfort
in the thumping pulse of techno beats,
Zorro's sword has been bested
by the fluttering of an Amazonian butterfly's wings.

Previously published in the Scarlet Leaf Review.

Magdalena

She sits surrounded by the trophies of a long life;
picture frames, china dolls, and mother's drapes.
The postcards she sent herself from some other world:
"Wish you were here."

Magdalena feels charcoal tears scald her scarred cheeks,
cut by Time's bloody scythe. She no longer recognizes
the hands that traveled the contours of her lovers' bodies.

Arthritis claimed her gnarled tribute long ago. Gasping,
she lifts her tired limbs from a clear plastic-wrapped couch.
Magdalena's knees burn while she limps

her way towards an antique mirror in the center of the room.
It was a gift from a past admirer, one of many.
Avoiding the accusing stare from her youthful portrait,
Magdalena forces herself to look ahead.

Standing face to face with her grandmother is enough
to confirm that treasures fade. Her cross becomes heavier
and the ground floods out from underneath.
"This is not my life... Take me back..."

Don Juan

Quiet wonder seized me;
jarring sound and sense bequeathed me
by the muse of inspiration,
knocking all reason from my head
till it lumbered down and bled
at the mere sight of you.

Scarlet waterfall cascading
down Latin shoulders masquerading
as stone cliffs in jubilation,
preventing the passage of this drifter
to the Promised Land this Easter
at the mere sight of you.

Mistress of untapped desires,
heroes light their own funeral pyres
with your name as motivation,
taking the deity's attention
from this young pilgrim's elation
at the mere sight of you.

Previously published in the Scarlet Leaf Review.

Hide and Go Seek

You went readily into the night
with a boyish swagger and a set bottom lip;
armed with youth, charm, and Daddy's words.

You went readily into the night,
jumping rope and playing tag;
waiting for the unknown hand to deem you "it."

You went readily into the night,
catching fireflies to light your face,
giving birth to the shadows that now live beneath your eyes.

You went readily into the night,
ignorant of the knowledge that would change
everything.

Welfare State

I kneeled tonight and began to pray,
when the question came to mind: "To whom?"
Whether it be Iehova, Jesus, or Allah,
we have forgotten that their names are verbs and not nouns.
In a world where hypocrisy is mass produced
and marketed as diplomacy to eager consumers,
we have stripped "God" of job and title,
adding one more to the unemployment line.
It is better to forget that we have torn Heaven from our hearts
and that above us there is only rain.

Jarhead

I am the stroke of a sword,
swift, powerful, and deadly,
tearing through flesh for the will of the mob
until my own heart is hacked away.

I am the sand of the arena,
rough, dry, and blood-stained,
trampled on by a thousand sandals
lusting for the next kill.

I am the amusement of Caesar,
cheap, loyal, and expendable,
catering to his visceral whims
at the cost of my humanity.

I am not a man,
free, unshackled, and valued,
able to live among other men
with the ability to choose,

I wonder if,
in the generations to come,
one's life will still be bound to the thumb of Caesar.

Previously published in the Literary Yard.

Eulogy (Narrative Poem)

Why do we die? This question has haunted me from an early age, around the time of my grandfather's death. Death had never seemed so real, or impactful, until it hit close to home. There is, of course, the scientific explanation: Our bodies give out on us. Age will rip and tear at our carbon vessel until life can no longer be sustained. Maybe a disease was the catalyst in our departure from this world, or maybe some tragic accident mangled our bodies to the point where our essence quickly ebbed away into the unknown terrains of death. Bottom line, we are organic creatures, made of material that wastes away, corroding into nothingness.

This leads us to another question: Is death merely a passage to some sort of afterlife? The faithful across the board speak of "God's plan." Our deaths are caused by a higher purpose and our reward for being good or our punishment for being evil awaits us on the other side of the chasm. We die because God in his, or her, great wisdom has a better design for the human condition.

To look at this question from an emotional angle, we must consider the trauma caused by immortality and why this makes living forever impractical. If the entire population were immortal, then life would become a monotonous routine, a maze with no exits. None would find rest from the endless grind of the day-to-day. Now, if only some people were immortal and not all, then these poor souls would have to live while their loved ones passed on, assuming a deep emotional attachment to family and friends. Either scenario causes emotional trauma for the immortal population, making immortality impractical.

From an environmentalist standpoint, an immortal population would waste resources at an alarming rate, causing the simultaneous death of every other species and the environment. If we were, in fact, immortal, starvation with no death in sight proves to be an unpleasant prospect. The inclusion of death as a part of life ensures the maintenance of resource usage at a moderate rate, ensuring a longer life span for the human species. It could be said that death brings life to our children and so on and so forth.

The reasons as to why we die are many. There are countless theories and hypotheses created to explain this phenomenon. Perhaps all of them are correct, perhaps none are. The only clear conclusion to be had from all this pondering is that death is an inevitable part of life and that it will be continued to be studied and explained for as long as reason and man live as one.

Previously published in the Literary Yard.

Mother's Milk

I know a few things about my mother:
All of her wedding pictures are ripped in half,
my father is wrong, and she's obsessed
with low-fat mango yogurt.
When we watch Bambi, she holds my hand tight
and doesn't let go until the credits finish rolling;
that's my favorite part.

Previously published in Uppagus.

Awakenings

The afternoons I spent trudging towards the bus stop,
drenched,
lamenting going home,
are sepia-colored dreams I reluctantly put aside
when I wake to find her snoring,
her back to me, sealed in my comforter.
The phlegm is a dull brown streak as I rinse it down the sink,
along with the last vestiges of sleep from my face.
Same pants.
Same shoes.
Different shirt.
My morning lacks variety
and I shower to keep up appearances.

Lingerie

3:33 am is the worst hour.
Everyone I know is asleep or fucking;
they can't be making love, not at this time.
Myshkin preaches Dostoevski's dogma,
but only for a little while; I'm not fond of idiots,
unable to muster enthusiasm for someone else's ideas
on how I should live my life…
You know that.
You know almost everything except
that you don't know much at all,
with your cigarette tongue, your Walmart apologies,
and your Victoria's Secret sex.

Thanksgivings (Haiku)

Amber Polaroids
framed by snapdragon petals
document the Falls

spent flying, fighting,
atop Baba's woods crowing
at the smirking sun:

"Qué onda, Güero?!"
as light rays engendered the
freckles on your thighs.

Previously published in the Scarlet Leaf Review.

Canción Protesta Miamense

Afuera, otra tormenta.
El cielo color melocotón podrido deja caer piedras,
bombardeando sin piedad el excremento de pájaro
que adorna el Mazda de mi madre.

No reconozco nada.
Me he olvidado cómo hablar el lenguaje de mi casa.
Pienso en contratar a un traductor para pedir permiso.
Me da pena usar el baño,
pero me tomo libertades con el gabinete de licor.

El pan integral y el queso blanco
son mis fieles compañeros cuando la noche y el día follan
y se enredan en tremenda Kama Sutra.

El internet me da préstamos
para sobrevivir esta bancarrota de melatonina,
pero como cualquier hijo de puta,
me sube los intereses cuando no me doy cuenta.
Mi billetera está vacía, pero siento su peso
cuando me estorba al caminar.

Todo cuesta; hasta el meditar te quita tiempo.
¿Qué hay de esperar en una ciudad donde
se usa el Nag Champa para disimular
el tufo a marihuana?

Ya me imagino a Jesús jugando Monopolio
con Buda, Jehová, Ja, Alá, y el Sol, riéndose mientras pasa
por "Salida" y recibe $25 adicionales por sus servicios
cuando sus fichas terminan en el arca comunal.

El grupo entero bebiendo vino chileno,
sentados sobre nubes de malvavisco, tomando el día libre,
hartos de escuchar en la oficina
como cometemos imbecilidades en su nombre
cuando ellos no tienen nada que ver.

Y aquí abajo, la soledad tiene sabor
a vodka barata y a té de canela.

Previously published in the Acentos Review.

Miami Protest Song

Outside, another storm.
Our sky, the color of rotten peaches, rains stones,
mercilessly bombarding the bird droppings
adorning the roof of my mother's Mazda.

I don't recognize anything.
I have forgotten how to speak the language of this house.
I'm considering hiring a translator so I can ask for permission.
I'm uncomfortable using the bathroom,
but I take my liberties with the liquor cabinet.

Whole wheat bread and white cheese
are my faithful companions when night and day fuck,
entangled in a colossal Kama Sutra.

The internet provides loans to survive
this melatonin bankruptcy;
but, like any son of a bitch,
it raises the interest rate while I'm distracted.
My wallet is empty, nonetheless.
I feel its weight hindering my steps.

Everything is expensive; even meditation costs time.
What do you expect in a city where Nag Champa
is used to disguise the stench of blunts?

I can imagine Jesus playing Monopoly
with Buddha, Jehovah, Ja, Allah, and the Sun,
laughing as he passes "Go" and receives
an additional $25 for his services
when his token ends up in the Community Chest.

The whole group drinking Chilean wine,
sitting on marshmallow clouds, taking the day off;
sick of the office's water cooler talk,
hearing how we commit atrocities in their name
when they have nothing to do with it.

And down here,
loneliness tastes of cheap vodka and cinnamon tea.

Previously published in "Love Letters To The 305."

Selfish

We went out for ice cream
because it's easier than staying in that cramped apartment
and staring at you with nothing to say
but "How was class, Honey?"
"Did you have a good day?"
"What did you have for lunch?"
You can't claim it isn't tiresome to look at me,
knowing I'm somewhere else.
I'd rather be anyplace else than here,
not able to remember that one time in St. Augustine
where you didn't embarrass me with your lack of tact.

I'll tell you what I do remember:
I remember trying to sleep with you on my shoulder,
your drool decorating my chest in droplets.
I remember making a sandwich and almost taking a bite,
until I stopped to cut off the crust,
because you always want a piece of what I have.
Most of all, I remember the way the setting sun looked
reflected in your dollar-store sunglasses
as you drove away after our second date.
You've always been at your most beautiful
when you were leaving,
but now it appears you plan to stay a while...
you're being unfair.

Spring Cleaning

This carpet needs a thorough cleaning.
It ranks first on a list of things I've yet to do.
There's always a reason to stay in bed, to shower later.
Just five more minutes and I'll tune my guitar.
Five more minutes and I'll go for that run.
Sandy can wait for her walk
five more minutes.
I don't see the point in sex tonight
when I can masturbate tomorrow.

Building a Reputation

I've imagined my own death more times than I remember.
Each deathbed confession specifically suited for the woman
I'm leaving behind;
crafted for the maximum emotional punch.
There's something delicious about leaving someone damaged
because they care about you.
No one kinder, no one better.
Nothing sexier than removing the object of your attraction
from, say, the path of a speeding truck,
and then, taking her place.
No man could ever live up to that memory,
no matter how much money he has or how defined his abs.
When you strip life down to its essential core,
the only thing of value is how a pretty girl remembers you
and what she tells her friends.

Archaeology

I really ought to thank you,
but you remain so blissfully unaware
of the chain of events you've set into motion
by chewing on your hair in complete concentration,
that I don't have the heart.

Why press this burden of responsibility
on your narrow shoulders? Narrow but shapely;
soft like your hips probably are, like the rest of you surely is,
as sure as your skin tastes like ice-cold mango
and watermelon sprinkled with lime juice
on an August afternoon.

I've rediscovered the joy of cliché
and the universal truth of musicals;
the zero-g exhilaration of dialing a phone number
and the paralyzing second before pressing send.
These baubles of humanity were lost to me for half a decade;
buried among others like them,
under mounds of sleepless disappointment,
each layer of sediment more compact
with the pressure of pain-numbing time.

The passion that defined every aspect
of my overly dramatic life
was replaced with practicality and a sense of duty
that prevented me from feeling.
Now, after a single dose,
I have an addiction to the melatonin you produce.

The lines of your silhouette, so round and delicately soft,
fade into pastels and take on a scent that reminds me
of nothing I've known; inspiring a panorama within me
where I want to build a home. I envelop myself
in the hope that true beauty lies beyond
the skin that has awoken me.

Planters

During the north Florida winter,
an expedition for thermal wool
in the depths of my closet is in order.
A cold day in the sunlight is no good to me.
Unlike the row of white carnations
lining your mother's window,
I need more than photosynthesis to live.

Mother Road

I blink,
painful discomfort
caused by sitting too close
to the highway
(white lines
drowning
in an onyx sea).
We drive,
windows open,
cigarette dangling from his lips,
unlit.
The black Camaro,
undetectable shadow
on route 66.
Only Dylan,
blasting from our speakers,
gives us away.
Photographs on the dashboard
stained with coffee,
credit cards maxed out.
We're rediscovering America;
documenting it for posterity.

Reasons

Your car broke down on the Turnpike.
Obviously, this is why you couldn't text me back.
Dr. Schaffer has you grading an ungodly number of lit reviews.
No wonder you haven't had a chance to call me.
Your sister is in the hospital
due to an allergic reaction to shellfish.
Being there is more important than meeting me
for hot chocolate, even though you promised.
My friends are way off base when they tell me
no one is that busy.
I'd rather imagine what you're doing than know.

Queen of Ephyra

"Don't get too attached," you said.

You're a rock, darling.
A hard, jagged, impenetrable block,
relishing your individuality,
proud of your loneliness,
blind to the quarry around you,
filled with endless granite.

I've rained down upon you,
ebbed and flowed around your parts
only to cause a landslide.
Moving you is a Sisyphean task
as you constantly reject the erosion
and transformation of rebirth.

Primavera en Invierno

Estoy acostado,
esperando el milagro de tus caderas
caminando hacia mí.
¿Tienes idea de lo que has encontrado aquí,
en mis brazos,
cuando recorres mis venas con tus dedos de cereza,
escaso recurso en el desierto de mi temprana madurez?
Mientras espero a Dios,
tu sexo es suficiente para devolverme la fe.

Previously published in the Acentos Review.

Spring in Winter

I lie,
waiting for the miracle of your thighs
walking towards me.
Do you have any idea of what you found here,
in my arms,
when you run your cherry fingers over my veins,
a meager ration in the desert of my early maturity?
While I wait for God,
your sex is enough to restore my faith.

Declaración de Impuestos

Tu rostro me ofende;
constante recuerdo de lo imbécil que fui al creer
en las mentiras que me tejiste con tu lengua de seda barata.
Tres cuentos por un peso, y eso debido a la inflación.

Cometí el error de enamorarme
del monstruo de Frankenstein en tanga.
La ironía de tu vestido blanco al pie de mi cama
todavía no encaja con mis memorias.

Dicen que los ojos son las ventanas del alma.
Entonces los tuyos deben ser espejos,
reflejando todo y enseñando nada
porque no hay nada que enseñar.

Permíteme pedirte perdón por haber gastado tu tiempo
con estupideces triviales como el amor
y el deseo de entregarte un futuro no definido por tu pasado.
No me había dado cuenta que no sabes amar,
pero eso es tu tragedia y no la mía.

Mi tragedia es no poder sentir nada
excepto una constante furia que me envuelve como
la atmósfera a la tierra, cambiando el color de mi cielo,
debido a la gran concentración de monóxido de carbono,
gracias a la polución de tu saliva
y tus arañazos contaminados de morbo con placer.

Mi tragedia es preferir la compañía del fantasma
de quien fingías ser a los cuerpos de todas las demás.
No puedo saborear la soledad cuando
todavía siento tus labios de cereza podrida
recorriendo las venas de mis brazos,
robándome la sangre,
prohibiendo a mi corazón que siga latiendo
al menos que sea por ti.

Tax Return

Your face offends me;
a constant reminder of my stupidity at believing
the lies you wove with your cheap, silk tongue.
Three yarns for a buck, and that's due to inflation.

I made the mistake of falling in love
with Frankenstein's monster in a thong.
The irony of your white dress at the foot of my bed
still invalidates my memories.

They say that the eyes are the windows to the soul.
Then, yours must be mirrors,
reflecting everything and showing nothing
because there is nothing to show.

Allow me to ask your forgiveness for having wasted your time
with the trivial absurdities of love;
with the desire to provide you
with a future not defined by your past.
I hadn't realized you don't know how to love,
but that's your tragedy and not mine.

My tragedy is not being able to feel anything
except a constant rage, enveloping me
like the atmosphere around the Earth,
changing the color of my sky
due to a high concentration of carbon monoxide;
a result of your polluted saliva
and your contaminated scratches of morbid pleasure.

My tragedy is to prefer the company of the ghost
of whom you pretended to be instead of the bodies
of everyone else. How can I enjoy loneliness
when I still feel your rotten cherry lips
tracing the veins on my arms, stealing my blood,
forbidding my heart to keep beating unless it's for you?

Toujours, Méliès

Ships drifting aimlessly in space
have found a moon to light their course
for a new universe inside a cup of tea.
An unexpected paradise bookended
by "bonjour" and "fais de beaux rêves."

Previously published in the Scarlet Leaf Review.

Pays de la Loire (Ekphrastic Echoes)

I beheld you in the distance,
verdant façade draped in olive creepers,
scorched stone divided
monument to a regal lineage
of threshold spaces.

Standing in your open mouth,
I ran my fingers through your crumbling walls,
etching your story,
feeling the warm blood of your past
with my skin.

I could not dare to enter.
Enveloped in your smoky conifer veins,
you've forgotten me.
The realization is a brutish solace
below the canopies.

The crackling of your leafy cartilage,
echoing beneath the sole of my boot,
Candescent summer crowing,
yesterday's delights now damp ashes
choking my lungs.

Nostalgia is no longer enough;
emerald kisses glistening in the corners,
forest temple ruins,
memories hedged in thorny desire
better left alone.

Inspired by a trip to Les Folies-Siffait in Les Cellier, France and "Ruin of Tabby (Shell) Construction, St. Mary's, Georgia, 2018" from Floodzone by Anastasia Samoylova

Pays de la Loire (Ekphrastic Echoes I)

Better left alone,
memories hedged in thorny desire,
forest temple ruins,
emerald kisses glistening in the corners.
Nostalgia is no longer enough.

Choking my lungs,
yesterday's delights now damp ashes,
candescent summer crowing,
echoing beneath the sole of my boot,
the crackling of your leafy cartilage.

Below the canopies,
the realization is a brutish solace.
You've forgotten me,
enveloped in your smoky conifer veins
I could not dare to enter.

With my skin
feeling the warm blood of your past,
etching your story,
I ran my fingers through your crumbling walls,
standing in your open mouth

of threshold spaces,
monument to a regal lineage,
scorched stone divided.
Verdant façade draped in olive creepers,
I beheld you in the distance.

Inspired by a trip to Les Folies-Siffait in Les Cellier, France and "Ruin of Tabby (Shell) Construction, St. Mary's, Georgia, 2018" from Floodzone by Anastasia Samoylova

Pays de la Loire (Ekphrastic Echoes II)

I beheld you in the distance.
Standing in your open mouth,
I could not dare to enter.
The crackling of your leafy cartilage...
nostalgia is no longer enough.

Verdant façade draped in olive creepers,
I ran my fingers through your crumbling walls,
enveloped in your smoky conifer veins,
echoing beneath the sole of my boot,
emerald kisses glistening in the corners.

Scorched stone divided,
etching your story.
You've forgotten me,
candescent summer crowing,
forest temple ruins.

Monument to a regal lineage,
feeling the warm blood of your past,
the realization is a brutish solace.
Yesterday's delights now damp ashes,
memories hedged in thorny desire

of threshold spaces.
With my skin
below the canopies,
choking my lungs,
better left alone.

Inspired by a trip to Les Folies-Siffait in Les Cellier, France and "Ruin of Tabby (Shell) Construction, St. Mary's, Georgia, 2018" from Floodzone by Anastasia Samoylova

Pays de la Loire (Ekphrastic Echoes III)

Better left alone,
choking my lungs
below the canopies
with my skin
of threshold spaces.

Memories hedged in thorny desire,
yesterday's delights now damp ashes.
The realization is a brutish solace,
feeling the warm blood of your past,
monument to a regal lineage.

Forest temple ruins,
candescent summer crowing;
you've forgotten me,
etching your story,
scorched stone divided.

Emerald kisses glistening in the corners,
echoing beneath the sole of my boot,
enveloped in your smoky conifer veins,
I ran my fingers through your crumbling walls;
verdant façade draped in olive creepers,

Nostalgia is no longer enough.
The crackling of your leafy cartilage,
I could not dare to enter.
Standing in your open mouth,
I beheld you in the distance.

Inspired by a trip to Les Folies-Siffait in Les Cellier, France and "Ruin of Tabby (Shell) Construction, St. Mary's, Georgia, 2018" from Floodzone by Anastasia Samoylova

Crime et Châtiment

A mud-gray car dove into the river.
I stand on the banks, examining her IOU:
"Regarde-nous bien!" Over
my head, clouds gather under Heaven. The once blue

horizon bloats with rain. Thunder
is the empty boast of a godless sky, I know.
What use are suits of armor in a storm? They are impractical,
rusting under the water's constant drip;
water that makes it feasible for farmers

to harvest Jeanne Moreaus draped in curtains.
These Jeannes pout and pose; their noise
overlooked in Ovid's translation
of Nature into Man. Nature feeds this haze

and my view of the horizon is fading fast.
But look, in the distance one can almost make out the graves
of Jules and Jim. They were friends, now lost,
who sank together in the Tomis mire that sullied Ovid's

legacy. Drowned in muck, the car is gone. On the shore,
I've ceased to breathe, and suddenly, aimlessly, my knees
sink into the river bank. I've become the sun-glare
of this world's supposed constancy.

Potential Energy

The waters absorb the light, drowning
the shore strewn with garbage. A heron uses
an MGD bottle to triangulate its position
for a landing. It stares at the turtles from a grassy perch,
high as the walls of Troy.

The colors are ill-suited for mid-afternoon.
Too many egrets occupy the right side of the sky.
O Lake, you lack the nuance of a master's brush.
The egrets, off-white and refusing to hold their poses,
flap like forgotten pamphlets.

The herons have taken flight, the egrets as well,
leaving the matted grass. Some tan-faced men
picked up the MGD bottle, perhaps to be recycled.
Mosquitoes fill the air.
Even the sunlight has left the waters.

Previously published in "Love Letters To The 305."

Calabar (Found Poem)

Just before the sudden dark, when the sun
took a curve out of the horizon of sea, the clouds
left the sky a pure amethyst pink
outlined with rims of shining gold
and the snow-clad Peak of Tenerife blazing
with star-white light. In a few minutes came the dusk,
out of its cloud-bank gleamed the red flash of the lighthouse.

Our summer voyage terminated at Calabar,
terminated gorgeously in fireworks
and what not. The whole settlement, white and black,
turned out for the coming of Lady MacDonald,
doing her the honour to the best of its ability; an ability,
from my previous knowledge of Coast conditions,
far greater than I could have imagined!

The Governor was delightful! A Spanish naval officer
with a strong American accent clinging
to his words. He gave a most moving account of how
all his friends and acquaintances carefully explained
to him that being Governor was equivalent
to execution. During the outward voyage,
the stories told by the sailors confirmed these views.

Adapted from Travels in West Africa by Mary H. Kingsley.

High Noon

The star on his pleated vest is dull as the crane
pulls back, showing a lone man
in a deserted town. Technicolor rain drips

on my window pane, taking me out
of black-and-white Hadleyville and placing me
on a faded blue couch in Florida.

The microwave beeps. She must have forgotten
her tea after slamming the door
on her way out.

I watch the gun fight while stirring honey into the tea;
a hostage is taken, a man shot in the back.
My back aches in grudging empathy

while my phone rings on the table. I brush the hair
out of my eyes, admiring the mise-en-scène.
I am torn

between love and a classic movie. The raspberry tea is sweet
in my mouth as Garry Cooper throws his badge
into the dirt.

Photograph

When my mother was a child, she couldn't play in the yard
because of her mother's warning: "If you run around outside,
you might fall and lose your virginity."

On my father's first birthday, he was given a blue balloon.
For his second birthday, they filled it with air. On his third,
his father slapped his cheek; a doctor's son does not cry.

Decades later, they went to the same party.
My mother arrived by accident. She had gone
with her brother and his new girlfriend, hoping to show
off a white, pleated miniskirt she no longer wears.

My father arrived with his army buddies;
six men in uniform piling out of a steel-gray '81 Beetle,
wondering if they would get laid that night
while they combed their mustaches at the door.

My parents met by the punchbowl and danced
to "Copacabana." My mother, heartbroken
over the loss of a now forgotten love, found solace
in my father's awkward two-step
and in the way she felt in that skirt.

They fell into marriage.
A Captain is supposed to have a wife;
my mother wanted a different family.
On the day I was born, my grandmother snapped
a picture of them before my mother went into labor.

Siddhartha's Son (Pantoum)

Nag-Champa smoke surrounds my plastic Buddha;
the scented wisps caress his glossy belly.
Upon his throne, my desk, his dimpled grin
reveals the inner peace that sparks my envy.

The scented wisps caress his glossy belly
and burn my nostrils. Eyes open, Buddha's face
reveals the inner peace that sparks my envy
and induces an awkward lotus pose. I breathe in

and burn my nostrils. Eyes open, Buddha's face
is intertwined with mine. My calf cramps up
and induces an awkward lotus pose. I breathe in
slowly; acceptance fills my lungs. All life

is intertwined with mine. My calf cramps up:
My body was not built for meditation.
Slowly, acceptance fills my lungs. All lives,
like mine, are salmon caught in Indra's woven net.

My body was not built for meditation,
my mind wanders off. How can a modern soul
like mine be a salmon caught in Indra's woven net?
Our present rises out of past traditions.

My mind wanders off again; a modern soul sits
upon his throne, his dimpled grin unchanged.
Our present rises out of past traditions:
Nag-Champa smoke surrounds my plastic Buddha.

The Lion

It moves its paws upon concrete savannahs
lush with wild Milky Way wrappers. Ants gather
around the mounds of speckled droppings

while narrow-eyed boys suck on pretzels and watch.
The lion's eyes, veiled golden freckles
of honey, blink behind oxidized metal bars.
He nudges a lioness from her sleep. Annoyed,

she lowers her head. Children sing "Hakuna Matata"
off-key and the lion handler tosses down
raw chunks of meat, clicking his tongue.

Genesis Now (Found Poem)

Soon after the beginning, God created
the breakup. He told his first son, born of mud,
"I'm seeing other people. Ones who treat me
as a God. And you know what? I find it good."
So it was that the Lord abandoned Adam,
who turned to Eve for some companionship.

Eve and the snake sat by the river Pishon,
in the gold-covered land of Havilah
where onyx, grass, myrrh-colored bdellium,
and lust grew plentiful. And Adam saw
how Eve became enamored with the snake,
his fancy clothes, and his Miltonic diction.

Eve had no time for Adam's boring stories,
his leafy underwear, or his love of breasts.
Alone now, Adam learned that love is fickle
and conditional. The only pleasure left
to him was gardening, but he lacked the skill
to prune the thorny roses from the bushes.

Adapted from a short story by Sabato Visconti.

Sunshine State

The path is littered with lightning-charred stumps
leading away
from the jaws of the beasts. They are drawn to my scent
of sweat and guilt,
my pores throwing up a fear of mangrove islands.
If I had left these woods,
I would have never witnessed the black-bellied plover
shaking off the dew,
baptizing dead leaves; the safety of water
a compass against drought.

"Lasciate ogne speranza, voi ch'intrate." The plover takes off.
I'm left in the middle
of man-made levees feeding the wrong side
of the panhandle.
The beasts are gone; nothing is left alive.
Brown sawgrass falls
limp on all sides; to the plover all this
might spread out like a map

of Africa. Beatrice, I name the bird Beatrice,
with her onyx belly and fickle wings
flying toward the Florida sunrise
made famous by postcards:
"Wish you were here."
"Abandon all hope ye who enter here."

Inverted Seasons

Spring's birthday falls on September 23rd
in Peru, and mine as well, but in Florida,
I celebrate my birth with autumn's leaves.
When I turned 3, I learned to read without
my mother's help, though I had her read me stories
until I was 12. My condescending glare
developed early on when teachers praised
my parents and themselves for my achievements.
I don't believe that I discovered Pablo
Neruda, more that he discovered me,
and so began my love affair with words,
though we've decided to see other people,
and my disdain for anything I create;
my songs of despair have been written long ago.

Deborah

A month ago, I started seeing Debby;
she has marble-grey eyes and smells of strawberries.
On Saturdays, we drink hot apple-cider at Maude's,
listening to live sets of bossa nova and jazz. Maude's
suits us, but not like the darkness of my room. Debby
loves to lie on my bed and talk about Lennon and Strawberry

Fields while I tune my guitar. She suggested a "Movie Night,"
a sleep over at my place. My mother would call her forward,
but I feel she moves at a good pace. Snuggling,
because "The Shining" terrifies her. I'm all for snuggling,
though her screams in the middle of the night
excite me, her watery eyes focused forward

towards the screen. Next year, Debby will be a memory,
a blend of strawberries and grey eyes. Now, she just cries
beneath my duvet and I look at her, quietly,
while she reaches for my icy hand. Quietly,
she curls up into the fetal position and a memory
is built out of Kubrick's film and Debby's cries.

Miraflores

The wind off the Andes plays with my hair,
parting it to the side with the affection
of a mother greeting her long absent son.
Spanish and Quechua intertwine in a web
that looms over me as the Sun-God looks on.

I take my first steps off the platform
and onto the paved roads leading me to the ancient ruin
where my afternoons were spent.
Turning around, I curse softly;
dwelling on the past is not my policy.

Lima has its share of charm.
Today I'll allow myself a stroll down *Larcomar*.
Sipping *chicha morada*, I'll walk up and down
this golden street, stopping only
for my first *desayuno lurin* at *La Flor de la Canela*.

After paying the bill, I'll ask the waitress for directions.
*"Pasando El Rancho Restaurante, pe, Jovencito. Al final
de la cuadra, justo al frente de la tienda Argos."*
I'll tip her extra well and then steal a kiss,
pausing only to regain my bearings.

Finally, I'll arrive at my *Abuela* Milona's house.
I'll return to soccer balls, turtles with three legs,
and chicken coops on the third floor.
The *carapulcra* will be on the stove, burning,
just how I left it; the *claveles* still blooming in the garden.

I'll arrive just in time to find a car bomb
blowing apart my childhood...

Faded Parchment (Found Poem)

The country on one side was as the country
on the other, the lowering the sky the same,
the fierce sun the same, only there was a road at last.

I went down into the valley, along a road
bordered with flamboyant trees, all full
of flame-coloured blossom, as Nature made it.

There was nothing to mark the border
between the Gold Coast Colony and Togo! After
a short time we came to a preventive station.

As I passed on, my wonder increased. Here
was exactly the same country, exactly the same natives,
and all the difference between neatness
and slatternly untidiness.

Suddenly, the curtain of my hammock was whisked up,
and before me stood a bearded white man
in a white duck suit, a small red badge
in his white helmet—the Commissioner!

I had come into this country without a credential
of any sort, speaking not one word of the language,
and I wondered what sort of reception I would meet with.

His bungalow looked a home; round it grew a tropical garden.
The pathway through the grove was a leafy tunnel, flecked
with golden sunshine that told of the heat outside.

"Of course you stay with us," his wife said in the kindness of her hospitable heart, and then drew me a bath, though there was certainly no "of course" about it.

Adapted from Alone in West Africa by Mary Gaunt.

Marriage

Guess what... Mary got married and left for Spain.
What do you think of that? I hope that she'll convince
John the beard isn't working for him.

Do you know that I can't stand tomatoes anymore?
Not even dipped in hot Swiss Miss chocolate at 4 am,
amid reruns of *Kojak*. It makes me feel gross.

Does it bother you that your father walks less
and eats more these days? He has this little bulge of a belly
that makes him look like a rope with a knot in the middle.

I wonder if my mother is getting that cough of hers
looked at, don't you? It kept her up at night, staring
at the bed that still ferments my father's humidity.

Previously published in the Literary Yard.

Paradise Pancakes

I usher cadavers to their seats at the corner IHOP,
undertaking a $7-per-hour smile
so others can enjoy paradise with a side of pancakes.

Since the boss has bestowed upon me every perk
a manger has except salary,
I work myself to death. Besides,

the other servers on the graveyard shift need a constant vigil,
always cooking up some scheme to avoid
rolling up utensils and refilling coffee pots.

When my shift is done, I limp to my Chevy.
Its asphyxiated blue stands out
in the empty parking lot.

Driving home is the hardest part of my day.
My mind wanders between daydreams and sleep;
I don't know which I prefer.

*"Miami holds nothing for me. I never should have left Peru.
The rent is due, again. A new tumor, divorce hearings,
more bills… Renzo hasn't called in two days."*

I have a son who knows how I should live.
He learns from books, professors, and his father,
but ignores what I've taught him.

I need to feel he is still part of me, connected,
even if that means he'll die buried under the pancakes
offered to regulars with their coffee.

A Winter's Tale

I think that I will die in Gainesville in the winter,
where snow refuses to set hand or foot.
God has turned into another statistic,
begging for change on University,
where students congregate around the bus stop
to see cars sputter past Leo's Pizza.

Among the Quick-e-Mart's selections, random
and scattered groceries, I stood transfixed,
watching row after row of frat boys march
past the scar-faced man asking for a buck.
I handed him the dollar they would not
but kept the twenty for myself.

Maluokeakua is no more.
Outside the Quick-e-Mart, the marked man stands
without a sweater to cover his frame.
He hopes that honesty will improve his luck
and he holds up a sign for all to see:
"I'm not about to lie, buy me a drink."

Previously published in the Literary Yard.

January

The walls of my mother's kitchen were lush
with faded sunflowers
and my grandfather's portrait. He stood in our garden,
dark suit and no visible hair,
the Bible that would become mine clutched to his vest.
I was convinced his severe expression
was a result of his daughter's failed beef stroganoff:
my grandfather suffered the indignity
of hanging just above the stove.

I stared at him, that man,
until the time came to put him away.
I removed the portrait from its grave of sunflowers
and turned towards the room where my godfather waited.
He looped the tie I had struggled with all morning
around my neck and tied the effortless knot
I was too proud to learn.
We walked out the door, silently agreeing
there was nothing inside worth setting the alarm for.

The window into my mother's kitchen showed nothing.
The world beyond those walls went about its routine.
Day gave way to the moonless night
and crickets performed the *Moonlight Sonata*
to an empty garden. The wind blew upon this house
then right through its foundation,
changing the way my mother would cook for years.

Portrait

Did you forget the day I chose to leave
the confines of our mother's modest house
for father's, circa nineteen-ninety-nine?
Remember, we had some things to figure out.

Mother came back from work around six-twenty
and as a show of filial courtesy,
by five, the room I used to make my bed in
was turned successfully into a study.

Our father helped me carry out the boxes.
He loaded them up in the Ford alone,
but only I could feel their hefty weight,
clutching our mother's portrait to my chest.

This note will find you fifteen years estranged
from mother—too long. Try and remember now,
how proud you were to leave, how righteous. Yet,
her portrait never left your desk.

Rashomon

The woodcutter came home that evening,
bringing flowers for his young wife,
stepping to the beat of the hammering rain.

The wife awaited her husband's return
from the deluge in the forest,
stoking the fire with last week's batch of wood.

The beggar hoped to chance upon food and shelter
in a dilapidated shack,
finding relief from the raging of the storm.

This beggar was brought before
the Gates of the Dragon, accusing the woman
of murdering the woodcutter.

An old priest happened by the bloody shack
after the rain ceased, wanting to pay
his respects and found an infant, abandoned.

The woodcutter had also been forsaken, crying
as a priest handed him over to his adoptive father,
a woodcutter as well, while the rain washed away the land.

Divorce (Villanelle)

These twenty years were more than jumbled noise
composed of her clichés and sentiments.
My words would hurt her in a quiet voice.

I tried to imitate my father's poise
while lawyers showed him where his marriage went.
These twenty years were more than jumbled noise.

My mother knew that apathy destroys
a home's foundations, torn without consent.
My words would hurt her in a quiet voice.

She found me on the bedroom floor reading Joyce
and pled her case for Christmases misspent.
These twenty years were more than jumbled noise.

My mother pressured me to make a choice:
choose her or patricide, to an extent.
My words would hurt her in a quiet voice.

I packed my suitcases for Illinois
and left my mom a kiss she would resent.
These twenty years were more than jumbled noise.
My words would hurt her in a quiet voice.

Royal Palms

Miami's color pastiche spreads before me,
a beach towel of polyurethane and pastels,
while the water greets hipsters and Europeans
with the warm embrace of an expectant lover.

A convention of umbrellas to my left
warns of the toll the sun will exact on my already tanned skin.
The laughter of children and remixed salsa beats intertwine,
filling the air with a mutated *guaguanco*
while smartphones relax for a little while
inside waterproof bags lying dormant on a sea of sand.

Oceans join and the waves dance
with the skill of a jubilant but clumsy amateur,
white foam steps tripping over each other,
colliding with bathers,
leaving them soaked in pleasant aquamarine apologies.

An ad boat cruises by selling sunblock
as a flock of clouds gather for Sunday mass
in our hot-pink neon paradise.
May it last forever.

Previously published in "Love Letters To The 305."

Frette (Haiku)

Questions lingering
past lustrous perspiration;
white duvet rumpled.

Paris-Charles de Gaulle (Haiku)

Unicorn balloon;
wooden frames encase your eyes,
azure promises.

Sacré-Cœur (Sonnet)

Will you remember the push of the wind?
How it felt heavy on our naked backs?
The crowd upon the crowded steps did thin;
our bodies speeding past the vaunted plaques.

I missed you then as I miss you now, my love.
I knew Parisian streets would not preserve
the feel of your lips on my neck. The clouds above
Montmartre enjoyed displays of joy observed.

The sun with rays of golden light outshined
all beauty from the white self-cleaning stone,
in much the way that time undid the bind
between our hands enlaced, now worn to bone.

The world kept on; the autumn reached its end,
allowing for this moment to transcend.

Zoom (Haiku)

The video is on...
We can see your underwear...
Oh god, turn it off!

Blackbeard

Another round is ordered in your honor.
Stories are told of the great black bear;
his prowess, his commitment to the cause.
Memories stitched from anecdotes,
a blanket of altars and sage
that failed to temper the wind.
You should be here
workshopping this poem,
lighting fires,
braiding tales of camaraderie into your beard,
becoming less a symbol and more a man,
receiving the gift of age,
wasting away in joy
instead of preserved in our grief.

Barbanegra

Pedimos otra ronda en tu honor.
Se cuentan hazañas del gran oso negro;
de su destreza, su compromiso con la causa.
Recuerdos cosidos de anécdotas,
una frazada de altares y salvia
que no pudo templar al viento.
Deberías estar aquí
revisando este poema,
prendiendo fuegos,
trenzando cuentos de camaradería en tu barba,
transformándote, cada vez menos símbolo y más hombre,
recibiendo el obsequio de la edad,
consumiéndote en alegría en vez
de ser preservado en nuestro luto.

The Space Between

Green leather-bound soviet documents,
French pilot certifications,
Holy cards by the hundreds,
dozens of Swiss Army knives,
faded mortgage papers,
divorce proceeding files,
stacks of workout videos,
binders of photocopied flight manuals,
sextants and sectional plotters,
paper clips and sheets of Forever stamps,
the smell of old parchment scorching my nostrils,
black and white ID pictures on top of sepia photographs,
pressure cooker seals,
an outdated Dell laptop that can't hold its charge,
plastic model airplanes,
brittle exercise bands and a legless trampoline,
flight logs and diplomas,
Charlton Heston VHS tapes,
a busted paper shredder and a worn tennis racket.
These things and more fill up your study,
alongside your empty chair.

Modern Vitruvian

The air conditioner sputtered as it fanned
away the lingering scent of alcohol.
I shuddered as I felt shame creep up behind

me. She left with my coat, a clear signal
that only a tasteless fuck would wear otter
fur. What other trinket had I picked up in *Brasil*?

Maybe my answer lay in these murky waters,
drenched in the Machiavellian philosophy
of her sweat. Shaking off the cobwebs, I gathered

that this morning woke up and found me
decked out in the clumsiness of metaphor
and a shirt too thick for this country.

I searched my mp3s for Billy Joel's *"River
of Dreams,"* trying to remember if she was blond,
a red-head, or bald. I had no desire

to find her. I don't have the sand,
I told myself, to acknowledge how I've betrayed
Fernanda again. Tomorrow night, by our nightstand,

I'll stroke her long hair, noticing the milky way
it flows over my fingers. I'll say *"Eu pequei
no camino para o seu coração,"*

knowing what that would imply.

Previously published in the Acentos Review.

Adams Hotel (Ekphrastic)

A stroll down cotton-candy sidewalks
leads to the Adams' foyer,
where a bellhop lobbies for your patronage.
It's an art deco crap-shoot;
smooth walls and sharp edges providing low relief,
a symphony of reeding and fluting
filling the air with decorative spandrels.
Here, at the Adams Hotel, they have an invariance
under the transform, an immunity to change;
a reliance on saturation and depth for impact.
The starkest of blacks and whites entwine
with lavish taupes and creams in a checkerboard motif
daring you to make the first move under the Florida sun.
You can almost ignore the potholes eroding into a moat
beside the facade as you lean on a telephone pole,
avoiding splinters while you rest.
The geometry of symmetry is exact but taste is subjective.

Inspired by "Park Avenue, 2018" from Floodzone by Anastasia Samoylova.
Previously published in "Love Letters To The 305."

What Nature Has Wrought (Ekphrastic)

The brightness of man's hubris
shines atop uprooted palms reaching for the firmament,
silent in rebirth.

You and I look out different windows
as if the intransigent panorama would darken less
in one than the other.

The Earth will exact its recompense
for the parched ignorance of urban development
with a flood;

black water swells, etching a path,
driving mediocrity from the face of nature's perfection,
marred by sidewalks.

As if we needed shoes to walk;
as if we needed stucco, vitrolite, steel, or terracotta
to feel alive.

Inspired by "Pink Sidewalk, 2017" from Floodzone by Anastasia Samoylova.
Previously published in the BeZine.

After Sunset (Ekphrastic)

My hand cramps in my pocket, hoping for what I don't expect.
The sodden confirmation that I've misjudged you
and that you're the storm fills my horizon.
I remember.
Insecurities boiled the oceans between us;
your voice thundered accusations as I lay
battered on your shore. No shelter or solace.
A grave of roots, drenched.
Now, this understanding will live forever.
The sun nods a farewell with the hollow pledge of tomorrow.

*Inspired by "Sunset after Hurricane, 2017" from Floodzone
by Anastasia Samoylova.*

Steps (Ekphrastic)

Serenity:
another vice hoping for the fellowship of addiction
as surrealists ascend and devolve,
never knowing where to stand.
A banister no one touches, useless orthopedics;
the phantom limb of coral concrete
overlooking mist and reflections,
the ghosts of sentiment splashing
pebbles in the mind's eye, never blinking.
Doppelgangers hang in shadowed corners, biding time,
the veiled threat of love radiating from the stillness.

Inspired by "Staircase at King Tide, Hollywood, FL, 2019" from Floodzone
by Anastasia Samoylova.

To-Do List

Make love in French and sing in Spanish.
Eat *tortilla de papa* in Buenos Aires.
Run five blocks to your car to beat the rain.
Temper your temper with a smile.
Rest my head on your lap while you read on the futon.

Count our macros while drinking white wine.
Stay at that treehouse Airbnb you keep bringing up.
Kiss all of your tattoos, starting at the wrist.
Go geocaching to get lost.
Build a fort out of pillows and your mother's duvet.

Drink negronis by the Mediterranean.
Breathe in your laughter.
Take blurry selfies while you make that face.
Survive dinner with your aunt.
Wrap Christmas gifts with parcel paper and red yarn.

Argue less to listen more.
Have a picnic by Lake Zurich.
Compare stories from our childhoods.
Ride bikes along the Loire and visit castles.
Trace constellations using the freckles on your skin.

Dash through Madrilenian crosswalks.
Lay on the beach wearing matching sunglasses.
Choose our daughters' names.
Play my guitar while you play with my hair.
Travel back in time to that afternoon in Montmartre.

Pick up the laundry.
Visit my tailor and choose the right tweed swatch.
Listen to Nina Simone vinyls.
Watch *Before Sunset* on your laptop before it breaks down.
Pick up a carton of almond milk.

Stop blaming you for our problems.
Wake up late and then stay in bed anyway.
Plant a garden of lavender and grapes.
Live a thousand lifetimes.
Find you in each one.

Forgive myself.

Liste à Faire

Faites l'amour en français et chantez en espagnol.
Mangez de la *tortilla de papa* à Buenos Aires.
Courez cinq pâtés de maisons vers votre voiture
pour éviter la pluie.
Détendre l'atmosphère avec une blague.
Repose ma tête sur tes genoux pendant que tu lis sur le futon.

Compter nos macros en buvant du vin blanc.
Rester dans cette cabane Airbnb dans les arbres.
Embrasser tous tes tatouages, en commençant par le poignet.
Faire du géocaching et perdre notre chemin.
Construire un fort avec des oreillers et la couette de ta mère.

Boire des negronis au bord de la Méditerranée.
Respirer ton rire.
Prendre des selfies flous tout en grimaçant.
Survivre au dîner avec ta tante.
Emballer les cadeaux de Noël
avec du papier cadeau et un ruban rouge.

Assembler des meubles pour ton atelier.
Faire un pique-nique au bord du lac de Zurich.
Comparer les histoires de notre enfance.
Faire du vélo le long de la Loire et visiter des châteaux.
Tracer les constellations en utilisant les taches
de rousseur sur ta' peau.

Jaywalk à travers les passages pour piétons madrilènes.
S'allonger sur la plage avec des lunettes de soleil assorties.
Choisir les prénoms de nos filles.
Jouer de la guitare pendant que tu joues avec mes cheveux.
Voyager dans le temps jusqu'à cet après-midi à Montmartre.

Rendre visite à mon tailleur et choisir
le bon échantillon de tweed.
Écouter Nina Simone sur vinyle.
Regarder un film sur ton ancien ordinateur portable.
Voir de nouveau le soleil se coucher sur l'Atlantique.
Appeler ton père et jouer au tennis avec ta sœur.

Se réveiller tard et restez au lit malgré tout.
Planter un jardin de lavande et de raisin.
Pliez le linge et nettoyez le sol.
Vivre mille vies et se trouver dans chacune d'elles.

Me pardonner.

To Noah, After the Flood (Ekphrastic)

Do what I tell you and you will be spared, my boy.
You have no idea, how could you,
of man's moral corruption;
of the need for the cleansing baptism of the flood,
the reversal of creation.

But you,
you have found favor in my eyes
because your eyes are my eyes.
You are mine and forever will be;
your blameless piety my source of pride.
It is you who will perpetuate my line.
The genesis of all my wishes will spring forth
from the ark of your growing body.

What I want
for you is what will be
and you shall usher in a new era
of prosperity.

But you,
your spirit will outgrow your body
as you make your own choices—
as our covenant erodes into a broken promise.
Anxiety grips me at the thought of you
facing a world I do not control.
Nature's future protection against catastrophe
is never assured.

Still

Our rainbow connection will be severed
and you will eventually realize
how powerless I truly am
as the water laps against your neck.

Inspired by "Flooded Garage, 2017" from Floodzone by Anastasia Samoylova.

Nimuë (Ekphrastic)

Converts kneel so close they lose focus
and shape the moment into a topiary.

What else could I want
reflected in the soft contours of your silhouette

crowned by palm leaves;
braided headdress of the tropics.

Behind you, your people do all their writing in fins
as they lament their fortune

with hurricanes instead of tears,
constructing their tributes in burnt sienna

horizons. To drown in the ecstasy of turquoise
waters one must be determined

and exhale when the moon is warm enough
to retire the sun.

Make your pleasure my own—
the pleasure is in diving in.

Inspired by "Biscayne Bay, 2018" from Floodzone by Anastasia Samoylova.

Tea for Two (Ekphrastic)

Melancholic reflections ripple across a forgotten moment;
the marble baroque elegy of a Pope's kiss
gives mana to the ground, inundating meaning.

This rusted theater of the absurd, geometry's little joke, sinks
without the support of wooden trellises,
now scattered and rotting among the bay.

Your filigree crown, once threaded and ingrained
in evergreen archways, lies laced to a faded horizon
split by lightning, the indelible signature of a godless sky.

I drown in the tepid ocean of your egress, floating among
parapet walks and balusters while a plateresque Poseidon
watches, disinterested, bathing in hushed phrases.

*Inspired by "The Tea Room, Vizcaya Gardens, Miami, 2017" from Floodzone
by Anastasia Samoylova.*

Infinity Pool (Ekphrastic Villanelle)

The sun averts its gaze from this décor—
cerulean pools impressed on nylon shades.
Yet here, in paradise, we want for more.

Greenhouse emissions burn us to our core,
but luxury's temptation rarely fades;
the sun averts its gaze from this décor.

Pink neon paint jobs decorate the shore:
Flamingo roads, abandoned soul parades...
yet, here in paradise, we want for more.

More sex, more wealth, more idols to adore,
anointed gloss of silicone brocades;
the sun averts its gaze from this décor

of polyurethane and ethnic war.
Our temple doors enhanced with colonnades...
Yet, here in paradise, we want for more

while nature waits, bitter revenge in store
for selfish waste of gifted promenades.
The sun averts its gaze from this décor
yet here, in paradise. We want for more.

Inspired by "Water Shade, 2018" from Floodzone by Anastasia Samoylova.
Previously published in the Ekphrastic Review.

Painted Landscapes (Ekphrastic)

Emboldened by our cities,
we've uprooted Nature from the Earth
and painted a memorial in her stead;
preferring the artificial to the real,
misplacing our faith in steel and chain-link fences.
Our need for control blinds us to the truth:
We get our strength from the chaos.

Inspired by "Camouflage, 2017" from Floodzone by Anastasia Samoylova.
Previously published in the BeZine.

Around It Goes, Redux

Around it goes.
Round and round it goes.
Picking up speed it goes.
Up and down it goes.
Back and forth it goes.
Side to side it goes.
Through our sight it goes.
Past time and space it goes.
Down it goes.
Up it goes.
Lethargically it goes.
Round it goes.
Now, it stops.

Crow's Nest (Ekphrastic)

Birds... Pollock's specks against the sparse canvas,
assembled in impossible angles; wings taut, necks twisted,
ready to abscond barren perches at a moment's notice,
sparing no thought to what they leave behind.

They feel what we refuse to see, suffocated by white space,
sitting restless on a congregation of masts,
branches in a forest, splinters on the water's skin;
the space between the gulf and the bay swallowing the Earth.

Our senses prove unreliable as time's procession collects alms
of lives misspent watching the horizon; of hearing
without really listening, of taking without giving—
Death's arrival is always in season.

Inspired by "Mast – St. Petersburg, 2018" from Floodzone
by Anastasia Samoylova.

River Cruise (Ekphrastic)

Hidden in shadow, dark arms exposed to the sun,
he exists in the queue of threshold spaces;
the veins on his limbs, a roadmap of manual labor.

The fear of a place where he has nothing is tempered
by the fear of a place where he cannot return.
This is the dilemma of purgatory, of the death of the self
and the birth of the spirit.

Neon green hulls contain the promise of opportunity,
floating on uncertain waters, sunlight reflected,
taking the shape of hope.

Twelve hours on a clock-face, twelve months in a year,
twelve chances for a child of the twelve tribes of Israel
to build a life in a world of rusted-white carbon steel,
shaped by the hands of his brothers.

Inspired by "Miami River, 2018" from Floodzone
by Anastasia Samoylova

Hanging Gardens (Ekphrastic Acrostic)

Above our heads, growing unperturbed,
Negating the inconvenience of plaster
And concrete soil, a plant stands in defiance.
Structures of all types are built, but Nature finds ways
To wear them down, to overtake them;
Amassing patience to teach lessons in hubris.
Silent custodians of unwavering purpose
In a world that chooses domination instead of harmony.
Ancient knowledge that we ignore at our peril:

Seven wonders were gifted to us,
An ascending series of tiered gardens containing
Marvels of mankind's imagination: trees, shrubs, and vines
Overhanging, a large green mountain of mud among them.
Years from now, this white building will be
Long forgotten, the exact location of this pensile paradise
Overlooked by cartographers and priests.
Varying accounts will meld into rumor
And still the roots will remain entrenched to the Earth.

Inspired by "Painted Roots, 2017" from Floodzone by Anastasia Samoylova.
Previously published in the Bezine.

What We Will Become (Ekphrastic Ghazal)

A chance encounter, some turns of phrase, make, love,
for the perfect opportunity in which to make love.

Underneath the canopies, your skin radiates lavender
while the shade and tropical skies flirt and make love

to the palm leaves that frame this momentary lapse
of decorum, which I will continue to make, love,

over and over again if you'll have me as you did tonight;
the feel of your fingers on my neck as we make love

revives my nervous system, every inch of me takes root
and grips the terrain of your quarantined heart. Make, love,

grow this feeling into more than what it is now. The orchid
of a sentiment hides among the trees if you make, love,

an attempt to know yourself when you're with me, Ana,
among this lush paradise; our Earth where we make love.

Inspired by "Roots, 2017" from Floodzone by Anastasia Samoylova.

Purple Rain (Ekphrastic Haiku)

Verdant life breaks through
concrete; a violet sea bleeds
out, staining our shores.

Inspired by "Concrete Erosion, 2019" from Floodzone by Anastasia Samoylova.

Water Temple (Ekphrastic Pantoum)

Crystal blue waters conceal lush secrets
in chlorine depths, oxidizing bitter truths
while leaves, lush with life's eccentricities,
age and wilt steadily into bronzed rot.

In chlorine depths, oxidizing bitter truths
give way to the evolution of self and we
age and wilt steadily into bronzed rot;
as it was, as it has been, our detachment

gives way to the evolution of self and we
burn, contently, while we tan beneath the sky
as it was, as it has been; our detachment
builds a strong case for the mercy of frostbite

burn. Contently, while we tan beneath the sky,
while leaves, lush with life's eccentricities,
build a strong case for the mercy of frostbite,
crystal blue waters conceal lush secrets.

Inspired by "Pool, 2017" from Floodzone by Anastasia Samoylova.

Antigua Belleza

Bajo cielos caribeños,
latiendo al ritmo de los tambores,
descansa el corazón de Antigua;
acurrucado con el suave cantar de una marea
compuesta por zafiros, esmeraldas y susurros
casi casi pero no totalmente olvidados—
fantasmas corporales de antiguos amores.
No esperaba descubrir el divino tesoro de la paz
entre tus muslos de arena asoleada.

Tuve que encontrarte para saber que me hacías falta,
que te perdí sin tenerte,
que tu libertad me pertenece.

El verde de tus hojas florece cada vez más,
tejiendo una corona que santifica nuestros cuerpos,
bautizados en el cantar de los grillos al anochecer,
regalándonos su serenata para conmemorar que existimos.

Galley Bay

Beneath Caribbean skies,
beating to the rhythm of steel drums,
rests the heart of Antigua;
lulled with the soft singing of a tide,
composed of sapphires, emeralds, and whispers
almost but not completely forgotten—
corporeal phantoms of ancient loves.
I did not expect to discover the divine treasure of peace
between your sun-kissed mounds of sand.

I had to find you to know that I needed you,
that I've lost you without having had you,
that your freedom belongs to me.

The green of your leaves blooms more and more,
weaving a crown that anoints our bodies,
baptized in the crickets' song at dusk,
gifting us their serenade to commemorate our existence.

Canción para mi Padre

Qué equivocado estaba,
pensando que estoy solo si tú vives
en mi forma de ser, en las lágrimas derramadas,
y en cada sueño incompleto al despertar.
Cuando la tempestad rapte al sol de mi cielo,
me serviría bien recordar que todavía existes,
cuidándome desde el umbral entre la realidad
y la imaginación. Tus consejos, la oración
que mi corazón repite en la oscuridad sin saberlo:

Padre mío, estés donde estés,
santificado sea nuestro nombre.
Venga a nosotros consuelo.
No entiendo tu voluntad ni en la tierra ni en el cielo.
No tengo apetito para el pan de cada día.
Perdóname mis dudas, así como yo perdoné tu certeza.
No me dejes caer en desesperación.
Más, libérame de todo miedo.
Ayúdame a aceptar lo inaceptable.
Amén.

Song for my Father

How wrong I was,
thinking I am alone when you live
in my way of being, in the tears shed,
and in every dream cut short at the moment of waking.
When storms hold the sun hostage from my sky,
it would serve me well to remember you still exist
in the threshold space between reality and imagination.
Your advice, the prayer my heart repeats
unknowingly, in the darkness:

My father who art wherever thou art,
hallowed be our name.
Thy solace come.
Thy will is not understood neither on Earth nor Heaven.
I lack the appetite for our daily bread
and forgive me my doubts as I forgave your certainty.
Lead me not into desperation,
but deliver me from fear.
For thine is the fiefdom, the knowledge, and the peace.
Help me to accept the unacceptable.
Amen.

Adieu

Sitting alone at a seaside table for two,
I can't help but remember you as the waves crash
your name upon the surf again and again.
You'd love it here, embraced in the sun-kissed waters
of the Caribbean that were never your birthright.
France is a beautiful country, filled with the philosophy
of bohemian intellectuals that did all their writing
with quills dipped in wine, giving rise to a culture of fashion
and the most delectable cheese. It reverberates with liberty
and romantic bicycle rides along the Loire in the spring.
Its allure is undeniable and its seduction irresistible,
but it can be terribly cold there.

You'd love it here and I never brought you.
I'm past obsessing about what I could have done differently
to bring you a peace that wasn't mine to give.
However, I'd like to keep a memory of that laugh
that made my world stand still,
reverberating around us as you hugged my shoulders
while the tide pulled us gently beneath the sea.

To remember your little chicken strut that came out after
a bit too much champagne when you wanted to seduce me.
The feel of your hair on my face while you pulled me into bed,
your kisses decorating my neck as I gave in. Your eyes,
unspoiled behind sunglasses, quietly begging me
to stay here forever; the red stains of our sweat,
mixed with rose petals, bleeding into the bedsheets.

Canto à la Victoria

Enamorarme de ti es enamorarme en español;
es recordar la calidez del sol y el abrazo de mi tierra;
es probar el sabor del pisco y del aguardiente,
de la uva y del agave.

Enamorarme de ti es darle cuerpo a lo imposible;
es pedirle a Dios que pare la luna para hacer de esta noche
la eterna acompañante de tu belleza;
es rezar y recibir una respuesta.

Enamorarme de ti es seducir a la pasión;
es beber el movimiento de tus caderas,
sensual y acaramelado;
es renacer en la luz de tus ojos cuando ríes
y sacrificarme ante tus besos.

Enamorarme de ti es bailar con mi suerte;
es nadar en el océano de tu caos
y regocijar en el desorden;
es la sonrisa de mi alma liberándose de perjuicios
ante el olor de tu cabello.

Enamorarme de ti es el privilegio de la esperanza;
es recostarme en tus pestañas para alegrar tus lágrimas;
es sembrar un jardín de sueños y girasoles
para mandarte flores.

Enamorarme de ti es comenzar a amarme a mí mismo;
es construir un hogar en el espacio
entre tu clavícula y tu pecho;
es escribir un poema en el Caribe para que sepas lo que siento.

A Song to Victory

Falling in love with you is falling in love in Spanish;
it is to remember the sun's warmth
and the embrace of my native land;
it is to taste the flavor of pisco and brandy,
of the grape and the agave.

Falling in love with you is to flesh out the impossible;
it is to ask God to stop the moon
and make tonight
the eternal companion of your beauty;
it is to pray and receive an answer.

Falling in love with you is to seduce passion;
it is to drink in the movement of your hips,
sensual and caramelized;
it is to be reborn in the light of your eyes when you laugh
and to sacrifice myself before your kiss.

Falling in love with you is to dance with my luck;
it is to swim in the ocean of your chaos
and to rejoice in the disorder;
it is to free my soul's smile from its prejudices
before the smell of your hair.

Falling in love with you is the privilege of hope;
it is to lay down on your eyelashes
in order to delight your tears;
it is to sow a garden of dreams and sunflowers
and to gift you bouquets.

Falling in love with you is to begin to love myself;
it is to build a home in the space
between your collarbone and your bosom;
it is to write a poem in the Caribbean
so you know how I feel.

Carta à la Victoria

No te veo hace un mes. He visto la luna,
fija y serena, reflejada en innumerables atardeceres
y las olas en la marea de tu partida;
pero no a tu rostro de caramelo
ni a tus ojos de almendra tostada,
llenos de risa y sueños nacientes.
No siento el ritmo de tus caderas,
envueltas en piel canela,
palpitando al compás de nuestro andar.

Te veo volteando de lo que puede ser;
tu cuerpo presente y tu mente alejada,
pero no lejos, no, lejos no,
porque tú me reconociste en la alcoba
de tu querer herido.
Me hace falta la posibilidad de esa realidad,
donde tú y yo existimos en el mismo plano,
preparados para sentir lo mismo;
una realidad sin miedos ni cicatrices.

No te escribo para atormentarte... te entiendo;
me gustaría que todo sea tan simple como pedirte
que me beses, que juntes tus labios con los míos
y veas lo que veo:
las primaveras en París e inviernos caribeños,
la vida con sus problemas sin faltar soluciones entre nosotros,
las noches de brindis con mi vino y tu cerveza,
los infinitos regalos que te quiero dar para que vivas segura
que no hay instante que no piense en lo que te gusta.

Te escribo esta carta porque es tenerte cerca,
pensarte, reírme con tus chistes y bromas ingeniosas.
Es decirte que me gustaría darte tiempo
pero no me interesa lo difícil.
Me he dado cuenta que cuando el amor es del bueno
no resta, sino multiplica exponencialmente;
se pasa los días llenando tu cofre
con bendiciones y ofrendas de agüita de coco,
calmando la sed y refrescando el alma.

Me despido con todo el amor que poseo,
y con esperanza,
porque el amor siempre debería concluir con esperanza.
Espero te llegue mi mensaje a tiempo.

Sinceramente,
Tuyo.

A Letter to Victory

I haven't seen you in over a month. I've seen the moon,
fixed and serene, reflected in countless sunsets
and the tide of your departure;
but not your caramel face,
nor your toasted almond eyes,
full of laughter and nascent dreams.
I don't feel the rhythm of your hips,
wrapped in the cinnamon of your skin,
pulsing to the beat of our stride.

I see you turning from what can be;
your body present and your mind distant,
but not far, no, not far,
because you recognized me in the bedroom
of your wounded love.
I need the possibility of that reality,
where you and I exist on the same plane
prepared to feel the same thing;
a reality without fear or scars.

I'm not writing to torment you... I understand;
I would like for everything to be as simple as asking
that you kiss me, that you join your lips with mine
and see what I see:
springs in Paris and Caribbean winters,
life with its problems and us with our solutions,
the nights of toasts with my wine and your beer,
the infinite gifts that I want to give you so that you live safely
with the knowledge there is no moment
I don't think about what you like.

I write you this letter because it is a way to keep you close,
to think of you, to laugh at our jokes and witty banter.
It is a way to tell you that I would like to give you time,
but I am not interested in what's difficult.
I have realized that when love is good
it does not subtract, it multiplies exponentially;
she spends her days filling your chest
with blessings and offerings of coconut water,
quenching thirsts and refreshing souls.

I say goodbye with all the love that I have,
and with hope,
because love should always conclude with hope.
Hopefully you get my message in time.

Sincerely,
Yours.

Mazo

Mamá me dijo:
"No seas tan profundo.
Eres demasiado profundo, como el mar.
No la asustes con tu emoción abrumadora
porque cualquiera se ahoga en la marea de tu querer."
Con el mazo en la mano,
me sentenció a una eternidad de ser otro.

Gavel

Mother told me:
"Don't be so deep.
You are too deep, like the sea.
Don't scare her with your overwhelming emotions
because anyone would drown in the tide of your love."
With gavel in hand,
she sentenced me to an eternity of being someone else.

Pragma

Summer's last breeze flirts with the skin on my neck,
fondling the almost imperceptible indentation your lips left
on their journey down my collarbone.

One of an archipelago of moments lush with flora,
harvested for pigments to paint memories... of you, of us,
of what we were and what we weren't in the deepest blues.

Waves of sapphires crash down upon the scattered islands
of when I met you, when I lost you, when I loved you...
How I love you,

submerged in the space between seconds, gasping for air,
filling my lungs with instants before they disappear
this year or the next, tomorrow, tonight.

Now... the now pours through my fingers and scatters
the ashes of minutes long departed into an ephemeral sea.
You told me no one gets out of love alive and I won't.

Eros

Come on in, love. Put your keys down, hand me your coat,
and all of your clothes. Your favorite *Ouzo* is chilled,
waiting to pour into the depths between us this evening.

The minerality of the *grand cru* enveloped in your grasp;
an anise kiss reverberating, dry promises trickle sweetness
down my spine. I'll only be a moment,
dicing these figs into an abstract to perfume the night.

Keep the fire burning...
longer...

Let it caramelize with anticipation watching you
dance around our table, fueled by the percussion
of the *dimotiki* in our breath, ending with your hands
wrapped around my waist as I plate the *baklava*.

Sit with me, feast with me, live with me,
consume me. I've been expecting you all this time
and I'm famished.

Philautia

You must move forward.
Take what's left of bike rides in September,
moonlit bonfires by the ocean,
of her warm thighs before breakfast.
Take what's left and rebuild the frayed edges
of your self-esteem before it flutters away
into the nothing you feed whenever you pick
at the scabbed flesh of your misplaced love.

You deserve more than you accept.

Please, learn this.
You'll blink and these years will join the others,
lost and forgotten, breathing dust in the caverns of the past.
Stop focusing on the size of your muscles
and your body fat percentage, cursing your genetics
for making expectations a seeming impossibility.
Struggles are over; you've made it.

And if it all goes away, you will find a way... forward.

There's still life left to live,
to enjoy; moments to inhabit,
and affirmations to validate:
You are worthy. You are loved.
You are enough.

Previously published in "Glow: Self-Care Poetry for the Soul."

Daydream (Sonnet)

My love, by your side, time is nothing.
We are together and apart, youth and experience all at once.
My inhibitions, collected leather volumes bound by passion,
lost in the great library of poems I write to praise your lips,

your eyes, your scent, your strawberry-satin skin.
Each book a universe and you the linen-clad Sun,
feeding the Earth I live on. Warming me
as I bask beneath the only Divinity I've prayed for.

I love you in the way great mysteries are loved:
quietly, with excitement and full of expectations.
Curiosity holds court, demanding to know your secrets.

And thus, time evolves from nothing, sitting in silence,
contemplating your faded portrait, whispering in my ear,
asking for you, then telling me to forget.

Benched (Villanelle)

I struggle finding words that will compel you to stay,
beautiful woman, my honey-pistachio blended dream.
Come, sit with me by the moonlit bay.

Kiss me with the strength of all your wants, I pray
as I try to find enough charm within to warrant your esteem.
I struggle finding words that will compel you to stay.

I fear my hesitation has let our moment slip away
as you grow bored with tired banter. My silent scream:
Come! Sit with me by the moonlit bay!

But you smile at me, your eyes suggest I cease to delay,
and find the courage to implement this scheme.
I struggle finding words that will compel you to stay.

Our hands beg for the nudge needed to find their way
across this chasm I've let widen to such extremes.
Come sit with me by the moonlit bay.

I see you, love, and all my pretty logic falls in disarray...
but chaos breeds opportunity, a chance to redeem.
I struggle finding words that will compel you to stay.
Come, sit with me by the moonlit bay.

Rivers

I fell, comforted inside the fear I hold for you.
I'd rather feel dread than the nothing of
this world bare of the mountains of your skin,
a cruel topographical joke at my expense.

You vanish when I blink; I convince myself
these tears are here to lubricate my eyes;
they lack the hydration of your gaze,
the source of the laughing rivers of Eden.

And I am an atheist, denying the existence
of our connection three times before the dawn
finds me accompanied solely
by the desire I dare not name...

For fear of a world where you don't exist.

Souvenir (Sonnet)

I keep your memory with me,
my dear. I keep it in my heart along with
Saturday morning cartoons, my mother's hand,
and mulled wine.

Life can stop gifting me things;
it can start to take them away, but you...
you remain with me, my love, embedded in the oxygen
that fills my blood.

There is no place I've traveled to where you weren't with me.
No sunset I haven't seen through your sapphire eyes.
No kiss I haven't tasted if not from your lips, my sweet.

You sustain me, at a distance, during moonless nights.
Even in death, your love will be my resurrection.
My darling, I keep your memory with me.

Discrepancy of Desire

And despite the years, last night, I cried
because I couldn't hear you snoring softly next to me.
You, who would wait till I fell asleep to use the bathroom,
who would throw entire meals away
if the pasta wasn't al dente,
who would buy a gift bag
because you didn't trust your wrapping.

It was evidence that there were nights
when you loved me enough to just be.
A simple message of vulnerability, proof of life
from behind the boundaries of the perfection
you wanted to portray
and that impenetrable stoicism you showed the world
along with a defiant lower lip and clenched fists,
daring us to find a single flaw
which you loathed to the point of rage.

They were what I loved most about you...
and so, you resented me
because I would not be satisfied with a mask,
no matter how beautiful,
painstakingly crafted
by your determination and skill:
Porcelain, lavender, and rouge.

I loved the nose you wanted to reshape.
I loved the hair you wanted to dye.
I loved the languages you wanted to forget.

Both Ways

I prefer us this way.
Dating without dating,
walking side by side, but not hand in hand.
Flirtation and banter stopping just short of true intimacy.
Laughing knowingly when people assume we're together
because we are and we're not.
This way, we can have it both ways,
committing to non-commitment.
This way no one gets hurt while it hurts.

Brothers

Little brother, disregard your constraints. You find beauty in life when you ignore the ticking clock. Time is ongoing, incomplete, eternal. Experience the passage of time; honor it. We evolve between moments because we choose to. Use your time, give it value, live in the moment, choose a path from the infinite choices before you and close yourself off from the distraction of other paths. There is no other road but the one you're on.

Do not be ruled by the tyranny of "what if." Affirm the moment and, in doing so, affirm all of existence. Be lured by your senses. Build relationships. They're hard work, but it's work worth doing. There's an inherent romanticism in the amount of effort put forth to keep things going. When the old genre of romanticism can no longer sustain you, look for a new genre. You know you're in the right place at the right time when you meet the right person. Indulge in the sapiosexual experience of the enjoyment and sensuality of dialogue. Walk and talk with others as a response to death. Create.

Art changes as you change. Feel abandoned by its love in the moments between actions. People leave us, transforming excitement into longing and a desire to follow in the alchemy of meaning. The only meaning that matters is the meaning you create, not only in your identity but also in your identity in relation to others. Make the choices that determine who you are, without fear. All you have is now, little brother. All you will ever have is now.

Previously published in "Glow: Self-Care Poetry for the Soul."

A World of Grief

Blurred, gray horizons
obfuscate still life. Beneath
the sky, only rivers.

The wind bellows
curses, threats, promising rage,
delivering sobs.

Light shadows the lines
etched in lightning; clouds pouring
raindrops, drowning tears.

Soil and six feet deep.
Memories of what we were
interred; rooted death.

A world of moments,
and, buried in each moment,
a world of grief.

Lisboa

I'm exploring,
led by cobblestone roads asking to be experienced,
no longer searching for a missing piece.
I am whole.

Light reflected, God's glitter,
envelops the horizon
while the hard consonant sounds of European Portuguese
pull at my shoulder.

The tiled walls on every building
bemoan their histories of poverty and sacrifice,
birds of paradise...
This is the foundation of a people.

Turning a corner means opening a gateway
to another time, hidden in front of me
if I would only see, while the city whispers its secret
poetry in my ear.

Praha

They lie on the ground, side by side
in a twisted *balasana*
beneath overcast skies.
Red plastic cups precariously balanced
on dirt encrusted fingers,
immobile.
One minute, two minutes, five minutes,
ten minutes...
waiting on charity that may never come;
the stone quarry strength of Romani hope.

Bali

I thought the sea would be different.
The sand is, volcanic ash, blackened by progress...
but the sea is the same.
It followed me, here, of all places.

Solitude is a warm hug. To share this with you
is to dilute absinthe with vinegar... intruding,
unapologetically, abruptly,
without a second thought to my introspection.

I left you in Canggu with a kiss on the cheek
instead of how I wanted to: dripping sweat
and smelling of my cologne. I would miss you.
I would wonder where you are.

I would wonder who you were with.

I didn't come here for you. I came
to stage a coup on my ego. To escape
the shackles of corporate America and to race time.
To see if I remembered how to yield.

To You, Who Would Love Me

We have razed the plains,
we have raged against hurricanes
together.

You know me, though you deny it,
though you forget.
You, who have seen fields of carnations wilt around me
as the sun refused its light. You,
who are the strength of my hands,
my parasol. You, who will be with me at the end of all things
as I was with you at the beginning.
Our history is written in crystalline gold ink,
on pages of seersucker blue,
eternal and forever, until it ends.

You know me, though it pains you,
though you're filled with regret.
You, who would keep me in a box
woven from bergamot bark and cloves,
away from those would take advantage of my heart
with promises that fade away in sincerity.
You, who has protected me from myself despite myself,
who knows what trinkets tempt me, that I can be bought
with currencies of soft kisses and citrus.

You've known me, through it all, through this vignette.
You, who would love me. Will you let me be loved?
Will you allow me the privilege of experiencing joy
though it can be laced with hurt? You,
who are my protector, my jailer? Will you let me
find connections, lay down roots, draw mana from flesh
and water? Will you sacrifice safety for freedom?
Will you be vulnerable with me?

We have razed the plains,
we have raged against hurricanes...
and we will continue to do so,
together.

No Big Deal

I want to know you—
reach you inside this city

where the rain reflects sunlight
only on Monday mornings.

This journey has taken
over fifteen years...

Our paths diverged in parallel,
kissed by the fog of time

before they had a chance to join;
before you could share your stories.

I'm at a disadvantage,
hands tied by doubt and lace,

hindered by fantasies
of what you loved to the point of folly,

of how you got those scars
you absentmindedly trace with your forefingers.

My imagination is no help,
ready to romanticize the shape of you

in an instant. To adore how you purse
your lips as you pronounce your "R"s.

Ruffle me, ravage me, redeem me...
There are no safe words here,

in this city where Sunday nights
leave you thirsty for more.

More of your stories. Come,
lay down beside me.

Come, lay down.
Tell me a story.

Eastern Wind

The exuberance of youth drives boys headfirst into Ceto's kingdom, engulfed in Turquoise rhythms until only experience emerges, dripping regret. Here is where you'll find me. Sitting on the sand. Watching the waves' tenacity... waiting for you.

I trace the cracks on my inner lip with your tongue, admiring the narcissism of grief and the expanse of my own ego for thinking I got to decide when I was finished mourning the trips I took into the thrilling unknown for the feel of your collarbone.

I sit here, above the sand of eroded Septembers, waiting for you. To tell you that I am no longer seeking because there is nothing I lack. Instead I explore, traveling the world as I'm able while different cities embrace me, whispering their poetry in both ears.

I owe nothing and am owed nothing. I give what I want to give and receive what I wish to receive. This is the gift life has for me and the lesson I couldn't learn while I labored for your love: the world is chaos and expectations will kill you. Make your own way.

I wait for you, beneath the breeze, in gratitude for all that you were, for a moment, shaping the man I am and am becoming. I wait to tell you what I've learned: that you are enough, that you are beloved, and that I no longer wait for you.

Previously published in "Glow: Self-Care Poetry for the Soul."

The Last Word

The last word is a gift wrapped in resentment,
tied with the golden ribbon of unmet expectations.
A promise to our ego, that we are faultless and justified
in all we have done.
It is the suit of crystalline armor
we wear against reality's keen daggers.

The last word is a photograph encased
in a frame of memories, faded into nostalgia.
A dear friend, showing up when our bar is fully stocked
only to empty the pantry as they leave.
It is the brand of melatonin gummies we abuse,
exacerbating insomnia.

The last word is a bouquet of roses,
tied to a stop sign at the intersection of a forgotten avenue.
A message of hope in a bottle, somehow
managing to keep afloat as the tide of fear swells.
It is the audacity to whisper "again"
after emphatically declaring "never."

STILL

Renzo Del Castillo

Notes & Acknowledgments

Some of these poems have appeared in the following publications: the Literary Yard, the Acentos Review, the Scarlet Leaf Review, the Ekphrastic Review, *"Love Letters To The 305,"* and *"Glow: Self-Care Poetry for the Soul."*

Thank yous (editor, publisher, friends and families)

I would like to thank my family for the love and inspiration they have given and continue to give me throughout the entirety of my life. Our experience is in the DNA of these poems; this is our story. I would like to thank my godfather, Roberto Moreno, for sponsoring my student visa and bringing me to this country which has become my home. I would like to thank my cousin, Pablo Avendaño, for encouraging me to express myself through poetry all those years ago. I would like to thank Michelangelo Qui Mutat Fatum for pushing me to submit my work for publication, for having a detailed strategy for said journal submissions, and for believing that I would become a published poet even when I had ceased to believe it myself. I would like to thank my dear friends, Inigo de Amescua and Curtis Franklin, for their lovely forewords, for the years of laughter, and the fellowship they have blessed me with. I would like to thank my poetry family within the Miami Poetry Community for developing an environment of inclusivity where art and communication can thrive. I would like to thank Flor Ana and everyone at Indie Earth Publishing for providing me with an opportunity to publish my first poetry collection, exhibiting great care and support for the artistic process. Finally, I would like to thank everyone who has inspired me to pick up a pen and write down these lines; the past lovers and friends who've filled my life with pieces of themselves. You've given me the greatest gift of all: connection.

About the Author

© Íñigo de Amescua Fernández de Casadevante

Renzo Del Castillo was born in Lima, Peru, in 1983, and was educated at the University of Florida, leaving with a B.A. in English, specializing in Victorian Literature, and an M.A. in Mass Communications, specializing in Intercultural Communications. Renzo currently resides in Miami, but he prioritizes traveling in order to experience and be exposed to the tenets of other cultures. He strongly believes that it is through art that we find the divinity of truth, the pathway of communication with others; that through this connection we are made whole. While he has spent the last 10 years as an executive in the healthcare industry, Renzo has been previously published in literary publications such as Literary Yard, the Acentos Review, the Scarlet Leaf Review, and the Ekphrastic Review.

Connect with Renzo on Social Media:
@elrenz

About the Publisher

INDIE EARTH

PUBLISHING

Indie Earth Publishing is an independent, author-first co-publishing company based in Miami, FL, dedicated to giving authors and writers the creative freedom they deserve. Indie Earth combines the freedom of self-publishing with the support and backing of traditional publishing for poetry, fiction, and short story collections by providing a plethora of services meant to aid them in the book publishing experience. With Indie Earth Publishing, you are more than just another author, you are part of the Indie Earth creative family, making a difference one book at a time.

www.indieearthbooks.com

Instagram: @indieearthbooks

For inquiries, please email:
indieearthbooks@gmail.com